STARTING POINTS

EARTH

Kate Petty

Photography by Chris Fairclough

FRANKLIN WATTS

NEW YORK · LONDON · SYDNEY · TORONTO

© 1990 Franklin Watts

Franklin Watts, Inc.
387 Park Avenue South
New York, NY 10016

Library of Congress Cataloging-in-Publication Data

Petty, Kate.
    Earth / Kate Petty.
        p.   cm. — (Starting points)
    Summary: Examines the properties and uses of soil and describes
how it functions as both a home for plants and animals and as a
building material.
    ISBN 0-531-14098-9
    1. Soils—Juvenile literature.   2. Soil ecology—Juvenile
literature.   3. Geology, Economic—Juvenile literature.
    [1. Soils.]   I. Title.   II. Series: Starting points (Franklin
Watts, Inc.)
    S591.3.P47   1991
    631.4—dc20   90-31022
                                                              CIP AC

Series design: David Bennett
Model making: Stan Johnson
Picture Research: Sarah Ridley
Typesetting: Lineage, Watford
Printed in Belgium

Additional photographs: Ardea 18t, 26br; Chris Fairclough Colour Library 6t, 10bl,
11tr, 22c, 30t; Geo Science Features Library 21bl; Robert Harding Picture Library
20t, 20b; Hutchison Library 21tl, 22b, 23t, 27bl, 30b; Frank Lane Picture Agency
4-5, 14bl, 14t, 14b, 15tl, 15br, 26t, 26c; Planet Earth Pictures 15bl; Frank Spooner
Library 21br; ZEFA 6c, 10t, 10br, 11tl, 11, 15tr, 21tr, 27t.

Acknowledgement: thanks to Stella Chapman and
Betty Matthews for help with the garden.

CONTENTS

The Good Earth

...We have turned another acre,
There's another sowing in sight.
Now toiling team and shining share
Have cut the furrows clean,
Let Sun and wind, rain, frost, and snow
Refresh the earth again.

Good seed when sown shall spring aright,
If the tilth and the season be fair;
Plow deep, plow sweet all sluggish soil,
Turn cold and dark to the air...
Let fallows lie, break fallows up,
The rhythm of earth is blest.

Taken from a hymn by *Oswald B. Powell*

Beneath Your Feet

The earth beneath your feet is mainly solid rock with a loose covering of smaller rocks and soil. You can see the rock clearly in mountainous places, or jutting out from the sea.

Rocks are forever being worn down into smaller and smaller pieces by the forces of nature – wind and sun, rain and river, ice and frost.

If you look closely at a spadeful of soil you will see that finely ground rock is the chief ingredient. The brown part of the soil that holds it together is called humus. Humus is formed from the rotting remains of plants and animals. It adds goodness to the soil. You can see some dead leaves and snail shells which have not yet started to decay.

The soil is full of living creatures too. Worms, ants, woodlice and other tiny animals tunnel through the soil, leaving passages where the air can circulate.

There are many types of soil. Sandy soil is made up of large rock particles while clay is of finely ground rock particles. Loam soil is a mixture of the two.

clay

loam

sandy

Life From The Soil

Only plants can make the food needed by all living things.

All the food humans and animals eat comes, in some way, from plants growing in the soil or in water. Plants are the only living things that can make food. A plant's food "factory" is its leaves. The leaves use the energy from sunlight to make the sugars, starches, fats and proteins essential for life. Leaves also take carbon dioxide gas from the air and transfer it into life-giving oxygen.

The roots of a plant which anchor it in the soil also draw water and minerals from the soil. Moisture is drawn into the roots through tiny root hairs, up the plant stem and into the leaves. Plants store their surplus food and water in their leaves, stems, roots, seeds and fruits. Plants have a great variety of ways of doing this. Think of the many different types of plants and where their food might be stored.

Food From The Soil

Almost everything you eat is grown in the soil or comes from animals that feed on plants. A farmer's most valuable possession is usually the soil he uses to grow his crops. A wise farmer looks after his soil and is able to produce good crops every year.

In developed countries farmers use machines and fertilizers to make their work quicker and more efficient. Farmers in many areas of the world are not so fortunate. Human muscle power and animals are often the only aids to farming the land. Poor soil and lack of rain can lead to disastrous crop failures and famine.

Plowing breaks up soil and buries unwanted plants. The soil is then smoothed out, ready for the sowing of seeds.

Modern farmers spray crops with fertilizers and weedkillers to help them grow better.

Seeds are usually sown in neat rows. This gives their roots enough space to draw water from the soil and their shoots the necessary air and sunlight.

Farmers cannot control the sun and the rain! A crop still needs the right amount of each to produce a good harvest.

Crops cannot thrive well where the soil is poor or when there is little rain.

Combine harvesters can cut and process cereal crops in a fraction of the time taken by older methods.

A Miniature Garden

You will need:

- a 15 in x 15 in seed tray, or similar container
- enough small stones to cover the bottom, and a few large ones
- enough earth to cover the area to a depth of about 2¼ in
- a little potting compost
- a mirror for a pond
- sticks, string, etc. for fences and swing
- plants and moss or grass seed

Collect plants that will continue growing, such as tree seedlings (look around the base of a tree, especially maple and sycamore); sprouted beans and seeds; carrot tops; cuttings from potted plants (such as impatiens) or shrubs (such as forsythia); small wildflowers (but only from the garden) with roots; and a few rock garden plants, such as saxifrage.

Lay a base of small stones for drainage. Use the stones to landscape a hill or a rock garden.

Decide at this stage where you want to put your pond, garden steps and "vegetable plot." Do your planting carefully, using a little potting compost and a good spray of water.

Add finishing touches such as a fence and a swing. Put down some moss for grass, or sow real grass seed.

Everything in your garden should continue to grow. The sprouted seeds in the "vegetable plot" will soon be ready to eat. Water your garden regularly.

Earthy Habitats

Many creatures make their homes in the shelter of the earth.

A fox's home is called a den. The fox often takes over another animal's home and extends it. The strong smell tells you that a fox lives there.

About thirty rabbits live together in a warren. The females do the burrowing when more tunnels are needed. They sleep in "rooms" deep underground. Every warren has several entrances.

The mole has a soft coat which grows in both directions so that it can tunnel backwards and forward without rubbing its fur up the wrong way. Moles are almost blind because they spend most of their lives in the dark. Tunneling moles create molehills on the surface, which can be a nuisance on a lawn.

Puffins sometimes nest in old rabbit burrows on grassy clifftops. The puffin lays a single egg, which it then incubates for seven weeks.

Gophers – or pocket gophers – are little burrowing rodents of North and Central America. Like hamsters (who also live in burrows), they have cheek pouches for storing food.

A wombat is a burrowing marsupial (pouched mammal) from Australia. The wombat's underground home can be 100 ft long, but it is only 20 in in diameter.

In Britain the water vole is another name for the water rat. These animals live in holes dug in the river bank. They are as at home in the water as on land.

Animal Puppets

You can make all kinds of puppets of burrowing animals. One of the worm puppets is simply a sock with two button eyes. The concertina worm is made from two long strips of paper, folded one over the other at right angles until they make a concertina shape, and glued at either end. The points are made from paper cones. Glue sticks to the cones to make the worm move.

Glove and finger puppets

You will need:

- **felt, furry fabric or any other material that looks appropriate**
- **needle and thread**
- **cardboard, scissors and glue**
- **assorted buttons or ready-made soft-toy eyes and noses (from craft stores)**

For finger puppets, make a pattern from cardboard by drawing around your index finger. For glove puppets, draw around your hand with your fingers together and your thumb sticking out. Then make the pattern symmetrical by adding a "thumb" on the other side. Cut the cardboard about 1 in out from where you have drawn.

Use your pattern to cut two pieces of fabric. Sew them together, leaving the bottom open. You can sew finger puppets on the outside, but sew glove puppets on the wrong side and then turn them inside out. Sew or stick on eyes, noses, ears, paws and tails. Use the pictures of animals in this book for more ideas for puppets.

Worm Watching

Worm casts are usually all you can see to tell you that worms have been busy.

Worms, ants, woodlice and other small creatures that make holes in the earth are good for gardens. Their burrowing makes room for air to circulate. Worms eat the earth as they tunnel along and pass it out as worm casts. They also pull dead leaves down from the surface to eat. If you keep some worms for a few days, you can watch what they do.

You can house worms in a fish tank or very large jar. If you want to construct a narrow wormery where the worms are never far from the glass, you will need an adult to help you. The wormery is made from two sheets of window glass or plexiglass, each 12 in x 16 in; two 12 in and eight 16 in strips of wood, 1 in x ⅛ in; one 12 in and two 16 in strips of wood, 2 in x ¼ in. A frame with slots for the glass is made by joining the wood with white glue and panel pins.

Don't fill the wormery until it is where you want to keep it. Contrasting layers of soil, peat and sand will show the worms' progress most clearly. Place some dead leaves on top and put in about six worms. Cover the wormery with black paper to block out the light, so that the worms feel at home.

After a few days remove the paper and see what the worms have done to the layers of earth. When you have made all your observations, put the worms back where you found them.

The Riches Of The Earth

Beneath the surface of the Earth lies a huge wealth of rocks and minerals. There are over 3,000 different types and many play a vital role in our world today. Some are very common and are easy to mine while others are rare or difficult to mine. Many different ways are used to reach them – from open pits and deep mines to boreholes.

The world is now being searched for the most important and valuable minerals. People and countries can become very rich from the discovery, and mining, of some minerals such as oil, gold and gemstones.

Drilling for oil in Angola, Africa. Oil and gas are usually found deep underground and boreholes have to be drilled to reach them.

A coal mine in Australia. Coal is the fossilized remains of swampy forests that grew in prehistoric times. Coal is the most common fossil fuel and is also used to make other materials such as plastics.

An open-pit iron mine. Here the whole mountain is made of rock containing iron ore so it can be mined easily. Iron is the metal in most common use today.

Diamonds are the most prized gemstones and usually come from very deep mines. The main diamond mines are in South Africa, Zaire and the Soviet Union.

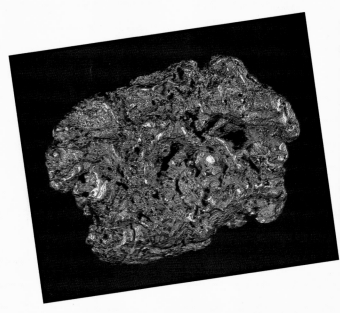

A gold nugget from a Russian gold mine. The largest nugget ever found weighed 472 lb. The largest gold deposits are in South Africa.

Panning for gold in Brazil. Some rivers contain gold washed out of gold-bearing rocks. Only very small grains are usually found.

Made From Earth

These bricks were made from a mixture of clay and sand.

The materials we build with come mostly from the earth. Buildings made from stone have stood for hundreds of years. Bricks also come from the earth. They are made from clay and baked – or "fired" – at a high temperature.

In hot countries many houses are built with bricks made from mud, which simply dry out in the sun.

Mud being trodden for plastering a mud hut in the Sudan, Africa.

Most of our plates and cups are also made from some type of clay. Clay is usually found in layers below the soil. Clays dug from different places contain varying amounts of minerals and can be quite different colors. Red clay, for example, contains iron oxide (rust is also iron oxide). Some clays can be fired at lower temperatures than others.

Earthenware pots are fired at a fairly low temperature. This village potter in India produces earthenware pottery. Here he is "turning" the pot on a wheel to make it round.

This bone china tea service is made from china clay – a very fine, white clay – mixed with bone ash. It was fired at a very high temperature.

Fun With Clay

Some ideas for things to make with clay.

You will need:

- **an apron**
- **a washable surface and an old dish towel to work on**
- **some clay**
- **a rolling pin**
- **a knife, pastry cutters, etc.**

These things were not baked in a kiln but just left to dry. They were coated with shellac and then painted. Only use shellac if there is an adult to help you. Enamel paint is the most effective, but you can use poster paints or even felt tip pens to decorate the clay. You can buy thread and fasteners for beads, backs for brooches and clips for earrings in craft stores.

Glorious Mud

Animals and people make the most of the healing properties of earth and mud.

These Sumatran rhinos are wallowing in mud to keep cool.

Elephants coat themselves with mud after they have washed and cooled down in water. The mud helps to prevent insect bites and cools them down some more. Elephants will spray dust over themselves to get cool when there is no water nearby.

Birds take dust baths to rid themselves of annoying small creatures. These birds are blue peafowl.

Fango is a mud from thermal springs in Italy. Bathing in it is supposed to be good for kidney problems and rheumatism.

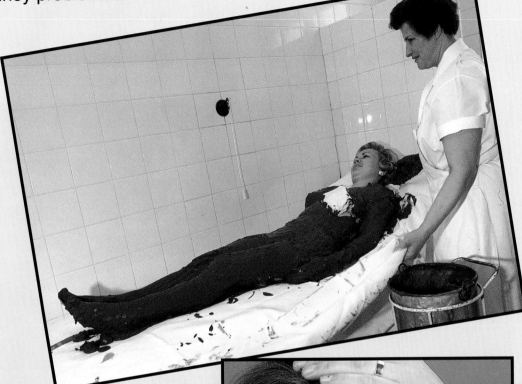

Sunabulo is the name given to a hot sand bath in Japan. The sand contains minerals that are said to have healing properties.

Mud from the Dead Sea is good for the complexion! Several beauty treatments contain mud.

Earth Pictures

The earth provides all sorts of things for making pictures with.

It can be quite a challenge to make a picture from such basic materials! Some stones already look like animals or faces; others can be painted. You can arrange stones in a tray to make a beautiful mosaic. The owl picture was made by sticking the stones onto stiff cardboard with Elmer's glue.

More Things To Do

Grow plants in different soils

Use three small flowerpots. Fill the first one with soil mixed with potting compost, the second one with sandy soil and the third with some sticky clay soil. Plant a few seeds in each and water them well. Put the pots somewhere that is warm and light, such as a windowsill. Water them every day. After about two weeks see which pot contains the healthiest seedlings.

Study some soil

Fill a jar with soil dug from near your home. Spread the soil out on a sheet of paper. Sort out the different things you find in it and list them. Feel the soil that is left behind. Try to tell if it is clay (sticky), sand (gritty) or loam (neither).

Test the soil for humus

Use three jars that have lids. Quarter fill one with sand, one with peat and one with soil from the garden. Fill each jar with water, put on the lid and shake it up. The soils will gradually settle on the bottom in layers. The humus will float to the top. Which of your soils contained the most humus? You can try this experiment with soils from your friends' gardens.

Digging for treasure

Archaeologists who excavate historical sites are uncovering layers of history as they dig. Some things are remarkably well preserved in the soil, such as the body of an Iron Age man found in a peat bog (known as "Pete Marsh," and on display at the British Museum, London), a frozen baby mammoth in Siberia, and Viking treasures that were buried with their ships. See if you can find out more about these particular discoveries. Visit an archaeological dig and watch the archaeologists at work. Some allow children to join a dig.

Collecting fossils

Fossils take historians even further back in time as they discover traces of prehistoric life in rocks. Fossils are formed when the remains of living things are covered over with layers of sand and mud which eventually, over millions of years, harden to become rock. Everything we know about dinosaurs has been discovered from their fossilized remains.

Fossils like this are called ammonites. They were formed nearly 200 million years ago.

Fossils found on the beach have broken away from the nearby rock. You can learn about life on Earth millions of years ago by looking at fossils. Make a collection and find out more about them – but take care: DO NOT climb cliffs or work where there is a danger of rock falls.

An earth quiz

1. What is humus?
a) ground-up rocks
b) mud
c) brown part of soil formed from decayed plants and animals

2. Which of these vegetables are "root" vegetables?
a) tomato
b) cabbage
c) beet
d) lettuce
e) radish
f) carrot
g) rutabaga
h) turnip
i) parsley
j) parsnip
k) pea
l) cucumber

3. Which of these animals are found only outside Europe?
a) red fox
b) rabbit
c) wombat
d) puffin
e) pocket gopher

4. Why are worms useful in the garden?
a) Because the birds like them
b) Because they eat the soil
c) Because their tunnels make room for air to circulate in the soil

5. What is coal made from?
a) fossilized trees and plants
b) oil
c) earth

6. Why might you have a mud bath?
a) Because it's fun
b) As part of a cure for an illness
c) To cool down

Earth words

What words would you use to describe earth? Think about the way it looks and feels, what people do to it and the different things they call it.
Here are some words to help you.

lumpy	crumbly	burrow	mineral	rock	compost
heavy	fossilized	dig	mud	sod	fossil
gritty	chalky	plow	land	sand	humus
rich	stony	tunnel	ground	tilth	earthworks
poor	boggy	excavate	heap	dirt	worm cast
marshy	slimy	mine	loam	muck	molehill
light	underground	turn	clod	ditch	hole
loose	soggy	bore	clay	trench	soil
dry	sticky	scatter	leaf mold	silt	
fertile	squishy	sieve	peat	furrow	
earthy	rocky	harrow	sediment	dust	

Index

Earth quiz answers

1. c   2. c, e, f, g, h, j   3. c, e   4. c

5. a   6. b

PRINTED IN BELGIUM BY

INTERNATIONAL BOOK PRODUCTION